A Quiet Walk in Central Park

A Quiet Walk in Central Park

EXPLORING THE BEAUTY OF A NEW YORK TREASURE

Written and Photographed by
FREDRIC WINKOWSKI

SILVER LINING BOOKS
New York

Produced and designed by Fredric Winkowski

For information address:
Silver Lining Books, 122 Fifth Avenue, New York, NY 10011

Library of Congress Cataloging-in-Publication Data is available on request.

ISBN 0-7607-2819-4

Printed in Singapore

987654321

First Edition

This book is dedicated to my family, so often my companions on those many enjoyable walks through Central Park.

Acknowledgments

Staff and volunteers of Central Park and the Central Park Conservancy. A special thanks to Regina Alvarez, woodland manager, for her extremely valuable assistance; Lydia Thomas, tour program director, and all the knowledgeable and helpful volunteer tour guides; Mary Habsteritt, gardener at the Shakespeare Garden; Paul Serra, assistant curator of the Conservatory Garden; Sara Cedar Miller, park historian and photographer; Vivian Antonangeli, for her advice; Barbara Morgan, my enthusiastic publisher/editor; Anthony Albert, director of the West Side Chamber of Commerce; Starr Saphir, bird identification expert; J. Christopher Muran, who introduced me to the mindful path; and to the great Zen poets of antiquity, who are a continuing inspiration.

Introduction

I'm one of those lucky New Yorkers who live near Central Park, and I've spent some of my happiest moments there, pushing a stroller, catching a baseball, or looking for birds on a beautiful spring morning. Cliché though it may be, Central Park is my backyard. Quiet and contemplative walks there are a simple activity, but one of the city's great underrated pursuits.

On the following pages, with photographs and some brief remarks, I examine and celebrate the joys of walking in New York's living treasure.

The park has never been more beautiful than it is today. The city and the Central Park Conservancy have restored much of its meadows and woodlands and lakes. This superb level of maintenance makes each visit a glowing experience, with endless opportunities for discovery as the moods of the days and seasons change.

I have explored Central Park with a camera and have been inspired and awed by its beauty. The

photographs in this book are a reminder of those moments. Along the way, I've also offered some suggestions that might enhance the enjoyment of a walk. The Zen-inspired verses scattered throughout point the reader to a slightly more mindful appreciation of the park's beauty. Central Park is always a pure pleasure, even if you stroll briskly through, passing flowers or birds with a casual glance. But—occasionally—stop. Really see the bird, acknowledge it and understand its existence on a deeper level. This is a slow and calming process and can make a quiet walk in the park even more rewarding.

Tranquillity

Tranquillity may be a state of mind, but in Central Park it is often a time of day. On a misty morning or a golden evening or after an afternoon shower, the park seems transformed into a transcendental garden. In the mist, the world is peaceful and timeless. The trees, the meadows, soften in the gentle light, and our thoughts become quiet. When we appreciate this silent beauty, tranquillity is everywhere.

Ah, yes . . .
this is my room.
Though it is not new,
it is my home.

As I stopped early one morning, looking at the twin apartment towers rising in the mist, an elderly gentleman approached out of the fog.

"Do you know the name of that building?" he asked.

I hesitated for a second, the name not quite on the tip of my tongue.

"It's the Majestic," he announced proudly.

Of course, how could I have forgotten, even for a second, the name of that magnificent building? It is, after all, the very essence of sophisticated New York architecture during the 1930s. So many other elegant structures line Central Park West, its residents drawn by the ever changing beauty outside their windows. There's the famous Dakota, sitting fortresslike on the corner of Seventy-second Street, built in an era when the Upper West Side seemed as distant and wild as the Dakota territory. There's the San Remo at Seventy-third Street, the Beresford at Eighty-first Street, the El Dorado at Ninetieth Street, all dotting the broad expanse of Central Park West, overlooking the boundaries of the park.

*Thank you,
misty sky.
Now I can see
more clearly.*

There are rare moments when the quality of daylight can be both subtle and eloquent.

One such moment came on an August afternoon, after a summer rain had ended. I was drawn to the park by a luminous glow. Everything looked different in the strange new light. Details that had previously been unnoticed now became visible; harsh shadows disappeared. The soft glow in the still, humid air bathed the entire park.

Here was a moment that showed clearly the unity of all things. Even the stolid statue of Daniel Webster radiated a sense of welcome. Although still in the shade, the willow trees billowed like soft green clouds.

the stillness of the lake

*Suddenly today
for the first time,
the water reflected
everything.*

The simple grace of the Bow Bridge shines in the perfect stillness of the Lake. Some say it is only here, standing on this old and beautiful bridge, that the skylines of both the East and West Side can be seen at the same time. The bridge itself is a marvel and a contradiction, a lacy froth of dense cast iron, built in 1862 to endure for the ages.

Generations of strollers have passed through this tranquil place, moving from the rocky wilds of the Ramble to Bethesda Terrace, the architectural heart of the park. It is a unique and lovely spot to stop and appreciate the continuing miracles of the park.

*Each morning
at first light,
each evening at dusk,
the water ripples
at the bird's passing.*

It was an unexpected early morning revelation. A snowy egret swallowing wriggling fish, one after another, for its breakfast, only feet away from Bethesda Terrace. Much too close to the trappings of civilization, I thought, for such an exotic creature. But I was wrong. The park, I would learn, is alive with birds. Some aquatic species even eerily imitate the commuting habits of New Yorkers, spending their nights on distant sandbars and flying into Central Park Lake to feed by day.

And as with many New Yorkers, the park is an essential haven for some birds, a place to stop and be refreshed. Each spring and fall the park is filled with migrating birds, who use its trees and meadows and lakes to renew themselves before moving on.

Some birds stay year-round—hawks, herons, mallards. For years, a pair of swans has hatched a new family every spring and chased the grown cygnets away every winter.

It is the natural dignity of these great birds and their grace that fascinates. Watching their deliberate movements and their calm focus somehow reminds us to slow our own pace and live in harmony with the pace of nature.

the lake, seamless and gentle…

The ducks and swans,
without a map,
know the way.
Teach me, swans.

As the afternoon deepened, the mist cleared slightly and the air became crisp. The fading sun painted Cherry Hill a subdued orange. Now the surrounding trees and especially the nearby streetlamp sparkled.

Part old, part new, the lamps glow throughout the park, their light changing as dusk dissolves into dark, now subtle, now sharp. The posts that support the lights are old, but the glass globes and metal housings are more recent, inspired by the French Art Nouveau movement of the late nineteenth and early twentieth centuries. While not a strictly accurate Central Park artifact, the lamps are attractive and add to the park's charm.

Life comprises many things, both the old and the new.

On one horizon
the sky is golden,
on the other . . .
I don't remember.

Turtle Pond revives from a limbo of neglect. During New York's lean years, in the 1960s and 1970s, this lovely and diverse marshland was hardly more than a forgotten patch of swamp. With more prosperous times, and a strategic location, came possibilities. The swamp's site, next to the Great Lawn and beneath Belvedere Castle, made it ripe for renewal.

Now the pond is reborn as a woodland marsh.

There is a dragonfly garden, an island for waterbirds, and plenty of turtles. Especially hypnotic is the wooden deck extending fifteen feet out into the water, allowing a close encounter with this aquatic refuge. A half hour quietly watching Turtle Pond can be as relaxing as an afternoon in Bridgehampton, minus the three-hour drive.

The prize is mine.
No one else
entered the race.

On a warm summer evening, waiting for the traffic light to change at Columbus Circle, you can sometimes feel gentle waves of cool air floating from the park. After the congested streets of midtown, here at last is a soothing refuge. Beneath the triumphant gilded statue, past the sidewalk café, people-watchers sit on the stone fountain.

Only a few enter the park at twilight. Those who do are rewarded with an unmatched experience.

With the park's activity level waning, the quiet walker finds that at last the park is his alone, or nearly so. If only that twilight hour could last forever. Sometimes on very clear evenings it seems to.

However, eventually the inevitable arrives. The park darkens; mystery gathers around it like a wild medieval forest. Walkers still on the emptying paths move faster, hurrying home before the night comes.

Beautiful Flowers

In Central Park, flowers reign; they are the jewels in the park's crown. Trees and shrubs are merely the background for the exuberance of blossoms, especially in the spring. Like bees and butterflies, we humans are attracted to flowers. We seek them out.

In the park, no directions are needed for the quiet walker who wants to be surrounded by nature's colorful glory. Flowers are everywhere.

The sun and
the springtime,
I desire them, but
they are already mine.

One sign that spring has arrived in Central Park is the appearance of rowboats gliding on the Lake. Another is the blooming of the flowering trees. At Cherry Hill, the dazzling return of life never fails to astonish. The sun is warm again; the days are long, and the park shimmers in its new pinks and whites. There aren't enough days in the week to experience the beauty that is so abundant at the end of April.

For the walker exploring the flowers of the park, Cherry Hill in the spring is a wonderful place to start. Naturally, Cherry Hill has many examples of its namesake, the cherry tree. The previous two pages show a Yoshino cherry and forsythia. Here by the Lake is still another Yoshino cherry and a black willow. The willow is clearly budding now, but its small branches are green year-round. They provide a reassuringly springlike appearance even in the winter.

Late summer flowers cling to the water's edge across the Lake at Hernshead. On the right, the native ironweed plant.

Throughout the park, native plants are being reintroduced. Hernshead, a secluded and natural place, presents a special challenge to maintain. Lakeside growth is fine food for baby swans and ducks, and would soon disappear without protection. Low fences have been erected to protect the plants from tiny beaks. Even so, hungry cygnets have been known to find their way around the barriers and enjoy a tasty nibble. The turtle shown is a red-ear slider, the type sold in pet stores. This individual could be a descendant of a turtle long ago released into the lake by some New Yorker weary of caring for it. This of course is a practice not encouraged by the park.

left
The yellow flower above is the
sneezeweed, a New York native.
It is similar to the sunflower,
and birds are fond of its seeds.

right
The red cardinal flower pro-
duces nectar that is especially
attractive to various birds,
including the hummingbird.

left
The tall cattail is good cover for lakeside wildlife. The red flowers in front are ironweed.

right
Smartweed is sometimes considered a bother, while others prize its wild beauty.

*Yesterday I dreamed
of spring flowers.
Tomorrow I will
remember them.
Today I call them
my own.*

A patch of sixteenth-century English countryside magically appears in twenty-first century New York. It is the Shakespeare Garden. Wildflowers in abundance, plus rough-hewn benches and fences create an inviting informality. Flagstone steps wind through steep and twisting paths. It is a place for intimate plantings and quiet contemplation.

Taken in total, the illusion is convincing. It's easy to imagine a thatch-roofed cottage just around the next bend in the path.

Of course, the point of the Shakespeare Garden is that the trees, shrubs, herbs, and flowers planted here were all mentioned in the Bard's writing. To orient visitors, plaques with Shakespearean quotations are scattered throughout the plantings. Some of the flora to be found here might include tulips, peonies, grapes, hyacinth, lemon balm, mint, periwinkle, and magnolia trees, to name a few.

There is also a mulberry tree (on the previous page it is the tree farthest to the right) grown from a cutting from Shakespeare's own garden.

A Shakespeare Garden is too lovely to exist in only one place. There are several scattered around the country, including one at the Brooklyn Botanic Garden. The idea seems to have flourished in the 1920s and 1930s. Central Park's garden was planted in 1916 by New York's Shakespeare Society. Over the years, the garden was neglected and finally became overgrown. In 1975 two designers, Bruce Kelly and David Harnell, established the present garden, which is new in concept and design. Early on, the designers, using true New York street smarts, chose theft-resistant plants.

The Shakespeare Garden blooms with snowdrops from early spring until the cold weather arrives. At the left is a canna lily, which appeared in the garden for the first time in 2000. On the right is a flower with a properly medieval sounding name: monkshood.

flowers all around us

Do the trees and flowers
know me?
I've been here before.

The designer's vision here emphasizes horizontal elements to bring us back to earth, a conscious contrast to the vertical buildings of the city.

The picture at left looks over the Untermyer Fountain in the North Garden. The green hedges are Japanese holly. The white flowers in the center are star magnolia and on the side are crab apple. A purple-leaf plum, in a planting area between gardens, is shown opposite.

There is one spot above all others where flowers rule. It is the Conservatory Garden at 105th Street and Fifth Avenue. The difference from the rest of the park is striking. This is a formal garden in the European style, with flower beds, hedges, and paved walks. Everything is clipped and geometric.

The Conservatory Garden is an expansive place, with three separate areas: A North Garden, a South Garden (the magnolia tree on the right is in the South Garden) and a Central Garden. In the Central Garden is a large lawn, with a path, or allée on either side. These allées are lined with benches and shaded by a canopy of crab apple trees. After a long afternoon exploring the park, the shelter provided by these trees is welcome, especially since the Conservatory Garden has a microclimate and can be a little warmer than the rest of the park.

Before leaving the Garden, think of this entire area under glass, because until 1934 it was. Before then, what is now the open-air Garden was covered by a large greenhouse, or conservatory. Budget cuts and structural problems led to the conservatory's demise and replacement with the beautiful garden we have today.

To gardeners, springtime usually means tulips. The Conservatory Garden is no exception. Here, tulips are the star of the show. During the preceding fall, forty thousand bulbs are planted to bloom in the spring. The tulips in the picture on the right are a low-growing, long-lasting variety named Princess Irene. They are named after one of the Dutch princesses and flower early in the spring. As the pictures on these two pages show, it would be hard to think of an area in the park with a greater concentration of vivid colors.

upper left
Bluebells near a tree on the
Woodland Slope.

upper right
Mixed daffodils (yellow and
white) with grape hyacinth below.

lower right
A bed of pastel-colored tulips,
with one red interloper, in the
North Garden.

lower left
Attractive foliage in the South
Garden, to be followed shortly by
a colorful display of tulips.

An Evening Walk

The evening was brisk and the cherry trees were in full bloom. It was springtime at its best. This was the perfect time to take the classic Central Park promenade, up the Mall to Bethesda Fountain.

As Central Park's creators, Frederick Law Olmsted and Calvert Vaux, saw it, this particular walk would be the ultimate experience of any visit to the park. The Mall and the Fountain are the architectural focus of the park, the destination to which all roads and paths eventually lead.

Two walkers seem to contemplate their next move as they stand at the south end of the Mall. This early in spring, there is an airy delicacy about the Mall not found later in the summer. The leaves are still new, and the evening

light can penetrate the long green canopy of elm trees.

Elms also line the east side of the park on Fifth Avenue. There are nearly one thousand elms in the park, highly prized and in need of close attention to ward off the deadly Dutch elm disease. Not far from the Mall, near the volleyball court, is perhaps the oldest tree in the park, a one-hundred forty-year-old English elm. Taken together, these trees constitute one of the largest stands of elms left in the country.

51

Running north, past the Bandshell, the grand straight path of the Mall halts abruptly (stopped by traffic lights and automobile traffic) at the Seventy-second Street Transverse. This is an unexpectedly low-key end for the majestic Mall. Even so, it is a pretty place, with its lovely, decorated stone pillars.

This particular location is the domain of skateboarders and in-line skaters. Skateboarders practice "ollies" and other tricks here. If a trick doesn't work, it's far enough away from the highly charged activity at the Bandshell that a little tumble doesn't matter.

On this evening, after enjoying the stroll on the Mall, it's time to cross the Transverse to Bethesda Terrace.

This cherry tree covering the world, it gladdens the heart of all people.

For many people, Bethesda Terrace is the very heart and soul of Central Park. It is the grand entrance to the natural world that stretches northward for the next fifty blocks. To live up to its role, Bethesda Terrace was designed as a grandiose place, like a stage set for a Verdi opera, with heroic stone fragments from a dreamlike Venetian or Moorish palace courtyard.

The view from the upper balcony is panoramic. The Lake, the Ramble, the Plaza below, and all of the park are revealed in one glance. The entire view is a Renaissance fantasy. Built in the mid-nineteenth century, when Gothic Revival was the dominant architectural style, Bethesda Terrace abounds in historical and allegorical themes. The stone carvings depict natural motifs in various seasons, and the hanging banners are of medieval origin.

Bethesda Terrace with its Fountain is a place to linger and savor an extraordinary beauty. Visitors come and go, but time passes slowly here. This is a good place to look outward and discover peace within.

For me, this has been a walk over familiar territory. Because I live only a few blocks away, I think of this area of the park as my backyard. This evening I walk more slowly and look more carefully than usual. I have to remind myself not to rush, as I often do.

Sometimes I stand quietly, with no other purpose than to understand clearly what I am actually seeing. It is not just a case of making time to smell the flowers, but to go several steps further and introduce myself and shake hands with them. Of course, I usually have a camera, a wonderful tool to slow down a walker. But taking a photograph is not the point; an empty camera would serve the process just as well. The point is to see.

Finally, at the far end of Bethesda Terrace, I take the path to the left and follow it for several dozen feet. Three egrets skim low over the still surface of the Lake. One finally lands, and the others seem to disappear. Returning on the same path, I pass Bethesda

Fountain again and continue home.

Serenity

Water can soothe and heal the spirit, as well as inspire the imagination. How many of us have sat and gazed at reflections in the Lake in Central Park, looking for clarity or direction or peace?

The calm waters of the park are something we enjoy every day for their beauty, but we also need them at other times, for the serenity and inspiration they can give.

If you say you are lost, then I would say, "Now you have begun to find yourself."

Along the West Drive in the Seventies, trees obscure the view to the Lake. Suddenly, at Balcony Bridge a clearing opens up onto what may be the best view in the park. Winter or summer, there are always people on the bridge admiring the sight before them.

At no other spot in the park do the towers of midtown appear more dreamlike than from this vantage point, near West Seventy-seventh Street. Looking from a distance of a mile or two, skyscrapers seem reduced to the size of miniature castles in some fairy-tale land. From Balcony Bridge, the lush midsummer vegetation threatens to reclaim all of Manhattan. Nature is definitely in charge here.

And that's as it should be, because here, as in other places of serenity, it is nature that claims our attention. The concerns of the workaday world should be of little consequence. Here we are free to meditate on the grand panorama.

*Would you not call
this my home,
since from this spot,
I see the things I love?*

An early morning mist over the Lake obscures the distinction between today and yesterday. The towers of the Beresford apartment building on Central Park West dominate the view as they have for more than seventy years. This is the time traveler's view of the New York skyline. Since 1940, when the distant El Dorado spires were built, this West Side scene has remained essentially the same.

West Siders passionately love their glorious skyline just as it is, and major changes would be nearly impossible to make. Because this stretch of Central Park West has been declared a Scenic Landmark and a Historic District, it is unlikely that this view will be altered anytime soon.

Looking like a sun-
dappled Impressionist painting, the waters of the Pool
scintillate in the autumn
light. For many New

Yorkers, the Pool, at 102nd Street, and similar pools at surrounding locations, are the next best thing to taking a trip into the country.

The park's character changes beyond Ninety-sixth Street. There are no statues; famous landmarks are few and far between, and a hot dog vendor is hard to find. On a weekday morning with school in session, expect to experience nothing but untouched beauty and acres of quiet.

the swan's paintbrush

On occasion, things fall together with blissful ease. How wonderful when a swan suddenly appears, silently gliding past in autumn waters.

But it is even more wonderful when a single swan feather touches the Lake, parting the green surface. The feather has painted a picture for us to admire.

with the circling birds

*Now I know, if I try,
I can see
yesterday's sunrise.*

On warm summer weekends, the park is filled with activity. It is a rare Sunday afternoon that the quiet walker can find serenity at the Great Lawn or anywhere else.

There is an exception. The park nearly empties of visitors at the most beautiful time of day. Late in the afternoon, many people head for home just as the park is tinged with the golden glow of evening. Then it can be quite peaceful, looking down from Belvedere Castle during one of those long summer evenings. The mirrorlike pond creates its own special magic, bringing the colors of the heavens down to earth.

In a drop of rain,
or in the veins of a leaf,
I see the universe
looking back at me.

It's easy to see why Zen poets and artists revere simplicity in nature. So much can be said with what appears to be so little. All that is needed to fully appreciate our world (so the Zen masters suggest) is quiet attention.

In those moments of mindful awareness, a particular instant can acquire universal meaning. Here, the pond and the sky are one and the same. Later, perhaps the sky may be seen as the entire universe.

Although the floating plant stems have their own particular past and future, for us they exist only in this beautiful moment.

Quiet

A new snowfall in the park is always a time of enchantment. Clean and white, it makes the world new once again. On a cloudy day, the snow adds brightness to the winter drabness. On a sunny day, when the park is busy with sleds and every sort of winter activity, it resembles a brilliant scene from a Grandma Moses painting.

Merely walking on undisturbed snow is a wonder. The crunch of fresh snow underfoot announces a small adventure with every step.

Walking in this
great place,
I know I am at home
no matter where I step.

A cold winter with snow cover is perfect for the vegetation of Central Park. The snow protects against the chill wind and acts like a blanket, keeping the dormant plants warm. Oscillations from warm to cold, common in recent years, are far from ideal. Although all plant life is affected, they are especially bad for new plantings. The youngsters may be pushed totally out of the ground and then need to be replanted before they freeze in the harshness.

Doing all the planting and replanting are the park's frontline troops, the horticultural staff. Although it shrinks in size during the cold weather, the staff is still kept busy with a multitude of tasks: trees and shrubs need to be pruned, last year's leaves removed, new plants must be ordered, and so on. As a reward for this effort, each spring the park emerges from the snows of winter more beautiful than ever.

Within the tree,
though the snow is falling,
sleeps the coming spring.

Snow-dusted wisteria vines grip the wooden pergola at West Seventy-second Street. Within three or four months, winter will be a memory and the pergola will be adorned with heavy purple wisteria blossoms. On a spring evening, the strongly perfumed aroma of the wisteria is beautiful, though some may find it overwhelming.

In the wild, wisteria vines can run rampant, encircling trees and endangering them. But here in the park, this city-bred wisteria curbs its aggressiveness and grows only more beautiful.

A walk on the west side of the Lake is rewarding at any time. The views are lovely, partly because of the luxuriant vegetation, which stays on in some form all year.

Looking down toward the water from Balcony Bridge, the abundant fragmite is hard to miss. The fragmite is a tall and pretty water plant with feathery tassels on top. Unfortunately, the plants tend to take over their environment without pro-viding much cover or food for wildlife. But everything in nature serves some purpose, and in spring the red-winged blackbirds do seem to enjoy hopping between fragmite stalks. The picture on page 87 gives a good look at frag-mite. In contrast, a plant with good ecological cre-dentials, the nearby bay-berry, shown on the left, provides cover for water-fowl and other wildlife.

Near Strawberry Fields, on the right, berries of the jetbead are avoided by ani-mals, and survive into the winter.

whiteness in the sky

The flapping of feathers,
the bird flying.
What is your name, bird?

In the winter, it's easy to see what a haven birds have in Central Park. Flocks of gulls arrive at the Lake when it freezes, breaking the quiet with their noisy squawking. Along with several species of ducks, of which the mallards are year-round residents, the gulls spend their days loitering on the ice, enjoying the life of a scavenger. Seen from close-up, (scavenger or not) gulls are beautiful birds, as these ring-billed gulls demonstrate.

The Parks Department gets several calls each winter from alarmed citizens who fear that during especially cold periods, the resident swans are in danger of being frozen into the ice. Park personnel investigate, but it hasn't happened yet. Officials say that as long as some portion of the Lake remains unfrozen, the Lake can sustain its swans. However, birds that typically migrate south are in danger if they overstay their welcome; for them, the Lake can turn cold and hostile.

Acres of snow,
in the distance
I see my home.

While watching the frozen lake at sunset from the Balcony Bridge, I was surprised at how quickly night comes to the park during the winter. One minute the setting sun colors the icy Lake pink and gold, and the next minute the sun is gone. At nearly the same instant, in the distance, the reassuring lights of the Plaza Hotel come on.

Night also comes quickly for the wildlife in the park. During the day, ducks tend to congregate around the Oven. This is an area on the east side of the Lake with slightly warmer temperatures because of its sheltered position and orientation toward the sun.

With the sun set, the ducks, all in a flurry, head for the protection of the bushes on the West Side, where they spend the night.

Places

Finding quiet and lovely spots, perhaps unexpected and hidden places, is a reward for exploring new paths. But there are so many glorious landmarks in the park also worthy of attention. The quiet walker should never overlook the obvious.

*The circle,
never ending,
invites us on a
timeless quest.*

During Central Park's dark ages of financial neglect in the 1970s, John Lennon often visited a wooded area off Seventy-second Street, across the street from his home at the Dakota.

After his tragic death in 1980, Lennon's wife, Yoko Ono, created a living memorial to him at that location. Known as Strawberry Fields, this is a beautiful area of woods, a meadow, lawns, and this mosaic, situated in the center of a circle of benches. Strawberry Fields was one of the park's first restoration projects. Perhaps Lennon's memory was a catalyst for the park's current rebirth.

This location is a wonderful place for rest and reflection. Even though armies of tourists visit this spot every day, Strawberry Fields still retains an intimate feel.

After time spent with the wind, soon the mayfly seeks the moon.

Just plain fun, rather than a quiet walk in the park, may sometimes be your goal. If so, the Carousel and the Bandshell are two good choices.

The cool, dark, and cavernous interior of the Carousel, with its booming calliope and giant horses, is both a treat and an object of mystery to small children. How exciting it is. It seems as if the entire building and everything in it spins round and round.

The Bandshell on the Mall and the short paved area just to the west, sometimes known as the Dead Road, are gathering places for young adults on wheels. For them, nonstop action is what it's all about.

If I were to choose a starting point or an ending point for any walk in the park, it would be Bethesda Fountain. Set in the middle of the park, near Seventy-second Street, the Fountain and Terrace represent the essential spirit of the place. Here is architecture from nearly one hundred and fifty years ago that continues to stir the aesthetic imagination while still serving a practical role as a delightful and spacious meeting place for New York's cramped citizens.

Two well-known spots for children to congregate can be found at the nearby boat pond. The Hans Christian Andersen statue is a spot where storytelling takes place on some weekend mornings. And the statue of Alice is a magnet for children, a tempting if slippery place to climb.

If Bethesda Fountain is the center of the park, to me the boat pond is the center of the universe. This is an extraordinary claim, I know. But since watching six high-flying skywriting planes years ago inscribe a vaporous circle in the deep blue sky, with the boat pond, where I stood far below, as its center point, it seems to me there's some validity in this claim, at least to me.

The boat pond is a large watery oval lined with benches and completely surrounded by trees on all sides. It feels removed from reality and all its worries. This is an incredibly soothing spot for an hour's relaxation. It is also the location in the park to rent model sailboats. In my experience, it is also a fine place to fish for crayfish, using a bit of hot dog tied to a piece of string as bait.

*What a nest
built the hawk,
says the sparrow,
snug in her tree.*

When I first arrived in New York, I was awed by the city's memorable points of interest: the Empire State Building, the Statue of Liberty, and so on. One spot that especially captured my attention was Belvedere Castle. I suppose I believed a castle in the park had an aura of timelessness and a heroic conception that defied reason and utility. In other words, it was fun to have a medieval castle in the center of Manhattan.

The castle was built in the spirit of fun. It is a folly, a type of structure built in parks and estate gardens, with no reason for being other than the mystery and romance it inspires. As designed, its doors and windows were purely decorative and didn't open. The ramparts of the castle did serve as a lookout point to observe the Croton Reservoir, which at the time was located below, in what is now the Great Lawn. In

1919 the weather bureau established an observation station at the castle, and weather readings continue to be gathered there today.

*In the house
of many rooms,
I know my way, though
my eyes are closed.*

The enduring stature of New York City as a world capital depends on the greatness of its cultural institutions. The Metropolitan Museum of Art, as a major repository of our creative heritage, is by any definition one of the greatest. And of course, so is Central Park.

How fortunate that the Met and Central Park share the same Fifth Avenue address. These two institutions energize one another as a result of their proximity.

One of the most satisfy-ing ways to approach the museum is to walk from downtown, past the sail-boat pond, and continue northward. A walk past rolling hills and blooming flowers awakens the appetite for the feast to come.

A Sunday stroll through the park to the Met is a New York tradition; a secular celebration of human-kind's highest aspirations.

*Let me walk
among the trees,
as I travel softly
in a dream*

From within the interior of the Metropolitan Museum, the park assumes the role of a backdrop for the arts. Inside the rear of the museum and on both sides, the light and ambience of the park create a near-outdoor setting in several sculpture courts.

The imposing glass façade that shelters the ancient Egyptian Temple of Dendur is shown on the previous two pages. The ethereal white figure here is actually a nineteenth-century statue reflected in the glass wall of the American Wing Sculpture Courtyard.

During warm weather, the quiet walker might visit the museum's rooftop sculpture garden for a magnificent reminder of just how large and green Central Park really is.

Without a doubt, the most important place in Central Park is the park bench. That includes just about any park bench, anywhere in the park. There's a lot that can be done on a bench. A few possibilities might include just relaxing, reading, writing, people-watching, having lunch, napping, chatting, and . . . you name it. I especially like a shady bench overlooking a vista. Give me a good book, and I'm gone for the afternoon.

Situated like an oasis in the desert is the hot dog cart. Since a hot dog in the park is an all-American classic, why resist the temptation? I wouldn't.

The Park in Motion

Central Park is many things. A garden, a woodland, a passage. It is a place to walk in spring or sit and watch the leaves drift to the ground in autumn. A place to read a favorite book, or to glimpse the beauty of nature in the midst of the city. And for many, it is a place to play. In its fields and on its paths, among its trees and on its lakes, children laugh, dogs frolic, and grown-ups enjoy.

*Behind
the pink flower,
I see
the petals of the sun.*

One recent April, the weather had been cool and the blossoms on the flowering trees seemed to last an eternity. This at last was the perfect moment, dreamed of throughout the cold winter. If only it could last.

And unexpectedly, I saw that it would last. Here, the painter has not only captured the beauty of the day but she is also part of that beauty.

Across the road is a museum filled with paintings, but what can compare with this?

This is not the tree I knew, though nothing has changed.

The quiet walker may value the beauty of the park for its own sake, or as an invitation to discover tranquillity within.

Children, however, are not given to quiet contemplation. For them, the park means fun, adventure, and discovery. A long tree limb is an irresistible spot for climbing, despite the protests of responsible and tree-loving adults. These children, in their school uniforms, are intently embarked on a private voyage to the unknown.

Below, a small boy tentatively examines a very large model of the United States Capitol building. The model, made entirely

out of small plastic blocks, was part of a toy display at Cherry Hill.

Today
I've walked and walked,
and tomorrow,
I will walk again.

As soon as you cross the Bow Bridge into the Ramble, the park landscape changes. This might be the terrain of a woodland in upstate New York. The trails are narrow and winding, and the trees are close in. It feels like a wild place; there are even raccoons living among the trees.

Before the park was built, the Ramble was swampland. Today, the trees that flourish here are plane trees, black locust, and sweet gum, which can survive both swampy and dry times. Of course, much of the Ramble, like almost all of Central Park, is a gigantic work of landscaping. In the 1860s mountains of boulders, topsoil, and trees were transported on barges across the Hudson River from New Jersey.

While walking in the isolated Ramble, it's reassuring to have a friend along for company. Or four friends, like this busy dog walker.

a dip in the land

On my nightly cross-park trek home, I have several checkpoints. After I enter at Columbus Circle, these personal checkpoints are places where I can perch for a few minutes and enjoy the park.

One such place is the Heckscher Playground at Sixty-fifth Street. Partially hidden by a dip in the landscape, it takes a slight detour to get there. Perhaps because of its relative isolation, it seems as if time has bypassed this secluded oasis of sports. Squint your eyes, and you're back in 1940, attending a softball game. Tree-shaded benches, dotted around, encourage this dreamy enjoyment of the on-field activity.

At bat, waiting for the pitch, the batter seems to take on not only the opposing team but all of Manhattan.

Throughout the day, when the weather is warm, the waters of the Lake are alive with the activity of rented rowboats. But in the evening, silently moving across the water, a Venetian gondola often appears. Incongruous? Maybe. As we stand on the Venetian-style steps of Bethesda Fountain, after the rowboats are docked and only the gondola rules the water, what could seem more appropriate? And when viewed from another vantage point, its curved prow appearing beneath the Bow Bridge, the gondola is a thing of striking beauty.

Starting at the Boathouse, the appropriately dressed gondolier takes clients for a romantic half-hour tour of the Lake. This is a venerable tradition, introduced in 1862. Then, authentic Venetian gondoliers serenaded their passengers with Italian opera while poling around the lake.

*Always one to be shy,
today the spring bird
leads a secret life.*

For the novice birder, the words "tree-watcher" may be more appropriate than bird-watcher. There are a lot of trees and branches out there, and at first, it isn't easy to find the birds among them. With patience, and possibly the help of a knowledgeable guide, the birds do finally appear. Eventually, at least a few of those elusive creatures can be identified.

Central Park is one of the great bird refuges in the world. New York City and its environs sit squarely on the East Coast path of migratory birds, the Atlantic Flyway. Birds, exhausted after their nighttime flights, and finding themselves over miles of urban development, need a green refuge. The 843 acres of Central Park provide that haven. In the spring and fall, birds from hundreds of migratory species depend upon the park for their survival.

It's natural that birders are advocates of preserving Central Park's natural bounty. As well as the birding community, there are countless individuals and groups dedicated to preserving the park's living treasure. Without their commitment and effort, how very quiet and diminished a walk in the park would be.

Walking in this
great place,
I know I am at home
no matter where I step.

Words and Pictures

Along with my photographs, I have included short verses that amplify some aspect of the photographs' meaning. The verses have been written in the spirit, if not the exact form, of Zen haiku poetry.

The haiku poem is like a photograph taken without a camera. It is tightly focused and accurate, yet replete with mood. Even beyond the mood in haiku are echoes of passing time and the essential primacy of nature. Often the poems show the oneness of all things. They subtly encourage the close, thoughtful observation of natural beauty, which can open the door to deep relaxation, tranquillity, clarity, communion. It is in this spirit that I present the words and pictures in this book. A quiet walk in Central Park really is a simple thing; but how complex that simplicity is, and how much of a miracle